Oxford

International
STUDENT'S
Atlas

Skills Workbook

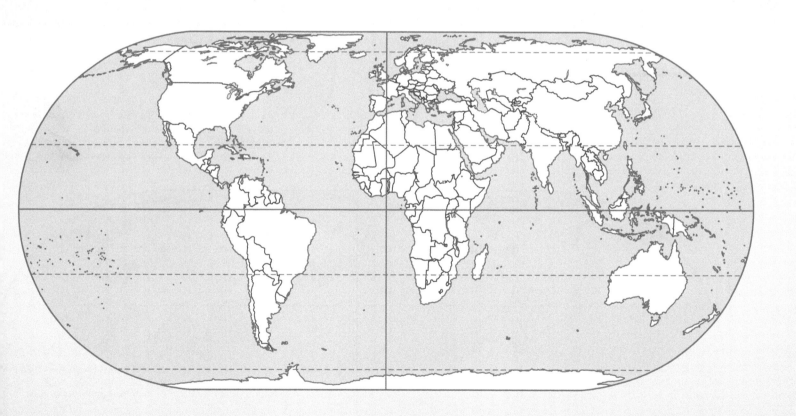

Name

2 Continents

1. Colour and label each continent on these views of Earth from space.
2. Using the same colours complete the map key.
3. Colour the map using the key. Label the continents on the map.

Key

- [ ] Africa
- [ ] Europe
- [ ] North America
- [ ] South America
- [ ] Asia
- [ ] Oceania
- [ ] Antarctica

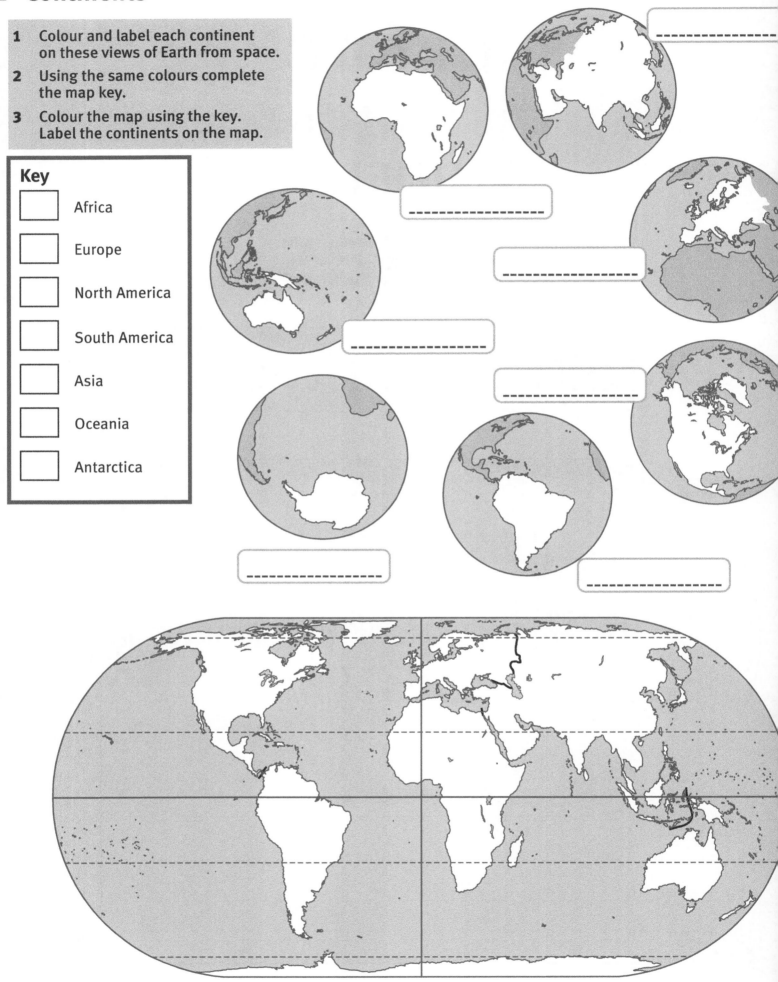

1 Label the following oceans on the views of the Earth from space. Some oceans appear on more than one view.

Southern Ocean

Indian Ocean

North Atlantic Ocean

South Atlantic Ocean

Pacific Ocean

Arctic Ocean

2 Label the oceans on the world map.

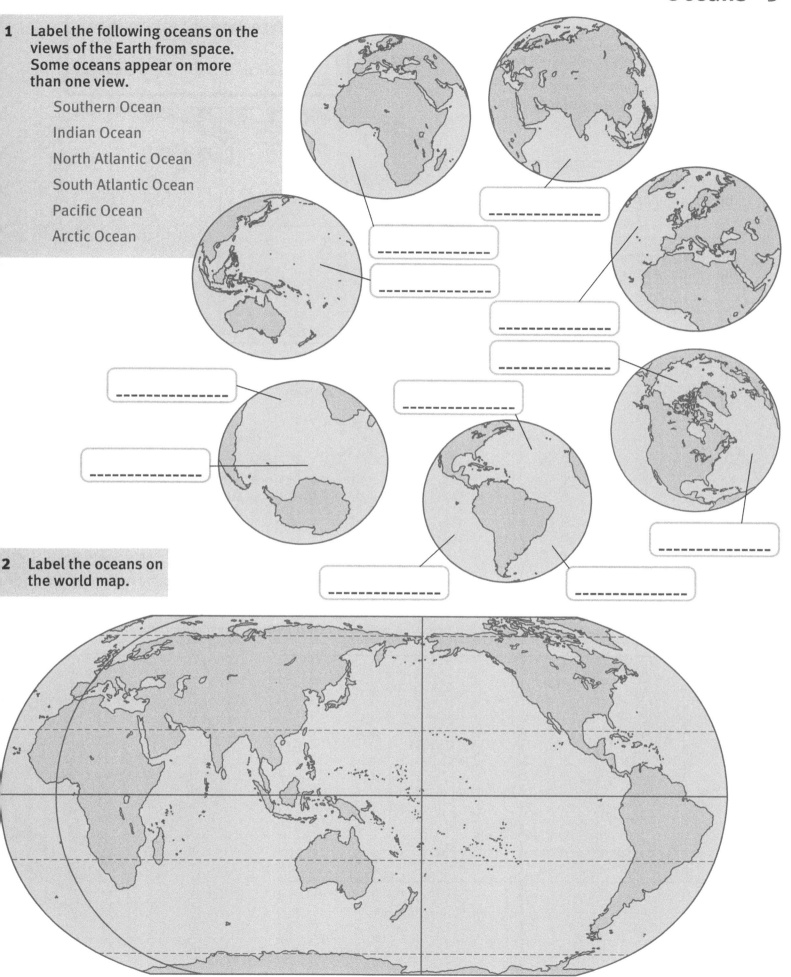

4 Map projections

1 Colour the key.

2 Using the key, colour and label each area on the maps.

3 Compare each map with a globe.

a) Which map is best for showing the shape of Africa?

_____

b) Which map is worst for showing the shape of Africa?

_____

c) Which map is best for showing the shape of Antarctica?

_____

d) Which map shows the relative sizes of Greenland and Africa least accurately?

_____

Key

| | Greenland | | Australia |
| | Africa | | Antarctica |

Eckert IV Projection (Atlantic centred)

South Polar Projection

Eckert IV Projection (Pacific centred)

North Polar Projection

Mercator Projection

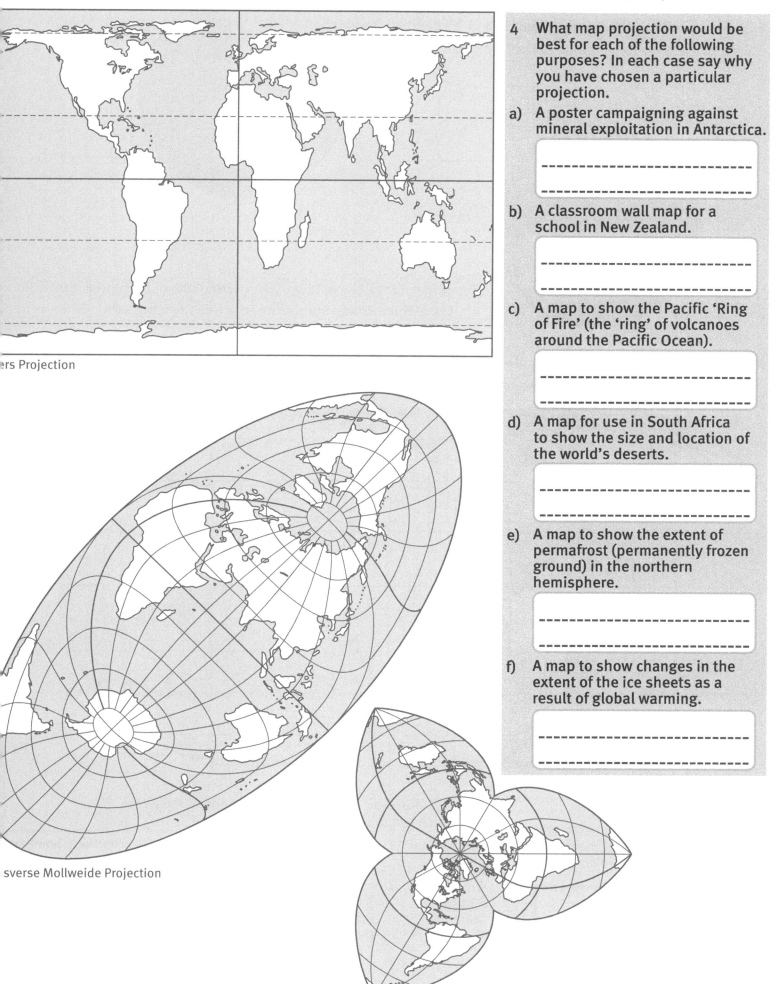

rs Projection

sverse Mollweide Projection

Tetrahedral Projection

4 **What map projection would be best for each of the following purposes? In each case say why you have chosen a particular projection.**

a) A poster campaigning against mineral exploitation in Antarctica.

----

b) A classroom wall map for a school in New Zealand.

----

c) A map to show the Pacific 'Ring of Fire' (the 'ring' of volcanoes around the Pacific Ocean).

----

d) A map for use in South Africa to show the size and location of the world's deserts.

----

e) A map to show the extent of permafrost (permanently frozen ground) in the northern hemisphere.

----

f) A map to show changes in the extent of the ice sheets as a result of global warming.

----

6 Latitude and longitude

1 These parallels of latitude are marked at 20 degree intervals. Label the missing numbers of the lines of latitude.

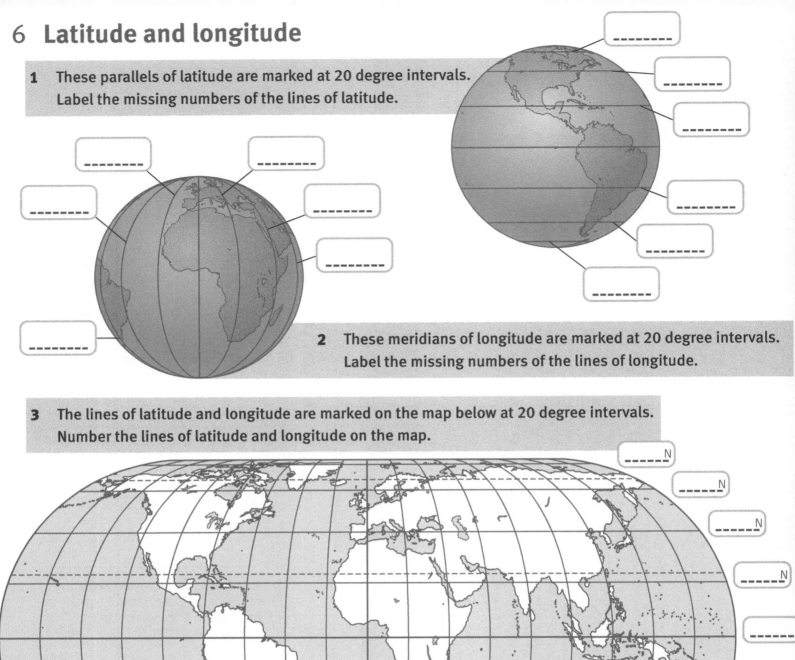

2 These meridians of longitude are marked at 20 degree intervals. Label the missing numbers of the lines of longitude.

3 The lines of latitude and longitude are marked on the map below at 20 degree intervals. Number the lines of latitude and longitude on the map.

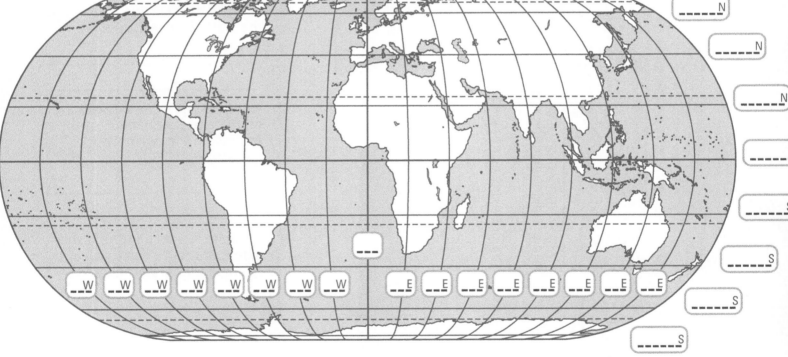

4 Colour the key.

Using the key, colour the land in the northern and southern hemispheres on the map.

Key

☐ Northern hemisphere

☐ Southern hemisphere

5 Which of these places are in the Northern Hemisphere and which are in the Southern Hemisphere?

Make two lists.

Johannesburg   Auckland
Washington DC   London
Beijing   Tokyo
Canberra   Buenos Aires
Anchorage   Nairobi

Northern hemisphere	Southern hemisphere
_____	_____
_____	_____
_____	_____
_____	_____
_____	_____

Some parallels of latitude have special names. Label them on the globe.

0°	Equator
23½°N	Tropic of Cancer
23½°S	Tropic of Capricorn
66½°N	Arctic Circle
66½°S	Antarctic Circle

7 One meridian of longitude has a special name. Label it on the globe.

0° Prime Meridian

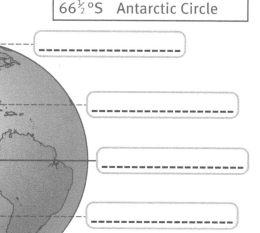

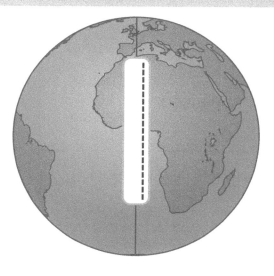

8 Label the special lines of latitude and longitude on the map below.

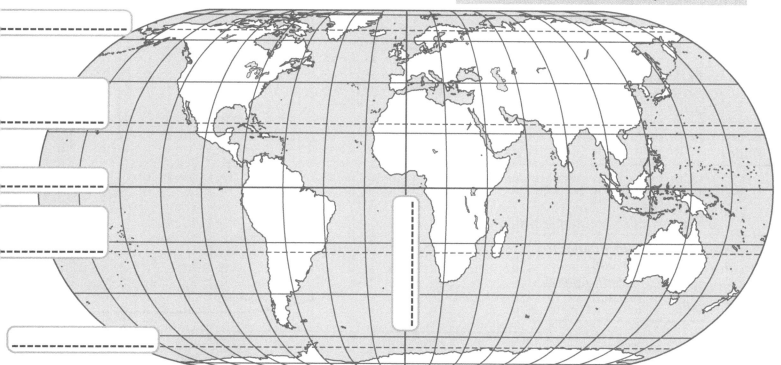

Mark where you live on the map with a dot.

Write the latitude and longitude coordinates for where you live.

latitude _____ longitude _____

10 Insert the missing words:

An imaginary grid is used to pinpoint the position of any place on Earth.
The grid consists of lines called p _____ of l _____ and m _____ of l _____ .

Latitude 0° is the equator and the other parallels are measured n _____ and s _____ of this line.

M _____ of l _____ measure distance e _____ or w _____ of the P _____ M _____ which is at longitude 0°.

8 World place knowledge

1 Label the following countries on the map. Use capital letters.

NIGERIA	CANADA
SOUTH AFRICA	UNITED STATES OF AMERICA (USA)
CHINA	
INDIA	
RUSSIAN FEDERATION (RUSSIA)	AUSTRALIA
UNITED KINGDOM (UK)	BRAZIL
	INDONESIA
	JAPAN

2 Mark and label the following cities on the map. Use sentence case letters (the intial letter in upper case and the rest in lower case).

Lagos	Beijing
Tokyo	Mumbai
Paris	Buenos Aires
New York	Jakarta
Sydney	Los Angeles
São Paulo	Shanghai

3 Label the following mountain ranges on the map. Use *italic* (sloping) letters.

Rocky Mountains   Himalaya
Andes

4 Label the following oceans on the map. Use blue *italic* (sloping) letters.

Southern Ocean	*North Atlantic Ocean*
Pacific Ocean	
Indian Ocean	*South Atlantic Ocean*
Arctic Ocean	

5 Find these countries on the world map. Label the name of each country and its capital city.

10 Europe place knowledge

1 Complete the map key.

2 Label these places on the map. Remember to use different styles of lettering for countries and cities.

FRANCE	SPAIN	BELGIUM	NETHERLANDS
Paris	Madrid	Brussels	Amsterdam
GERMANY	SWEDEN	ITALY	SWITZERLAND
Berlin	Stockholm	Rome	Bern
NORWAY	UKRAINE	LUXEMBOURG	
Oslo	Kiev	Luxembourg	

3 Label these features on the map using a different style of lettering for rivers and mountains.

Alps
Danube
Rhine

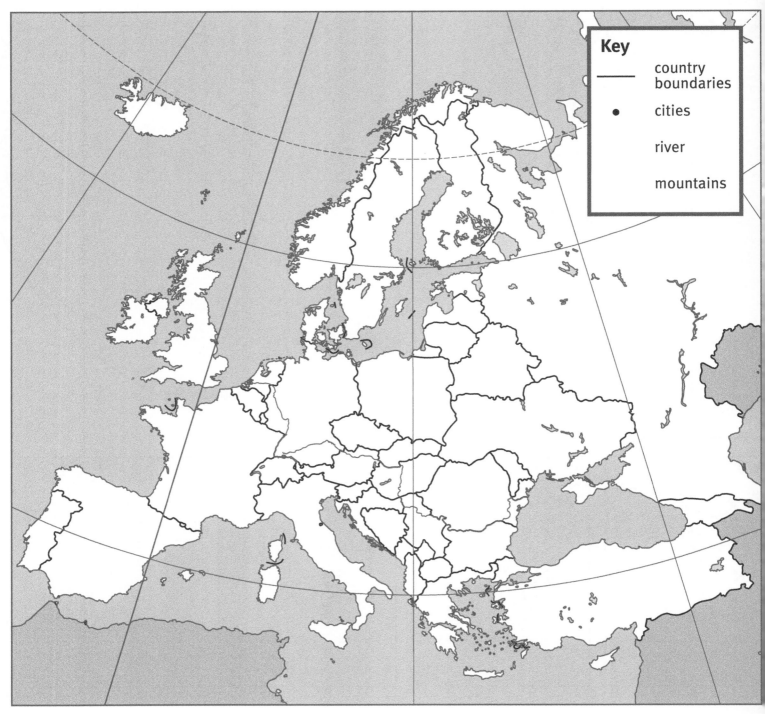

Key

— country boundaries

• cities

river

mountains

1 Complete the map key.

2 Label these places on the map.
   Remember to use different styles of
   lettering for countries and cities.

CHINA	INDIA	SAUDI ARABIA	TURKEY
Beijing	New Delhi	Riyadh	Ankara
RUSSIAN FEDERATION (RUSSIA)	INDONESIA	MALAYSIA	THE PHILIPPINES
	Jakarta	Kuala Lumpur	Manila
Moscow	JAPAN		
	Tokyo		

3 Label these features on the map
   using a different style of lettering
   for deserts and mountains.

Himalaya
Ural mountains
Gobi desert

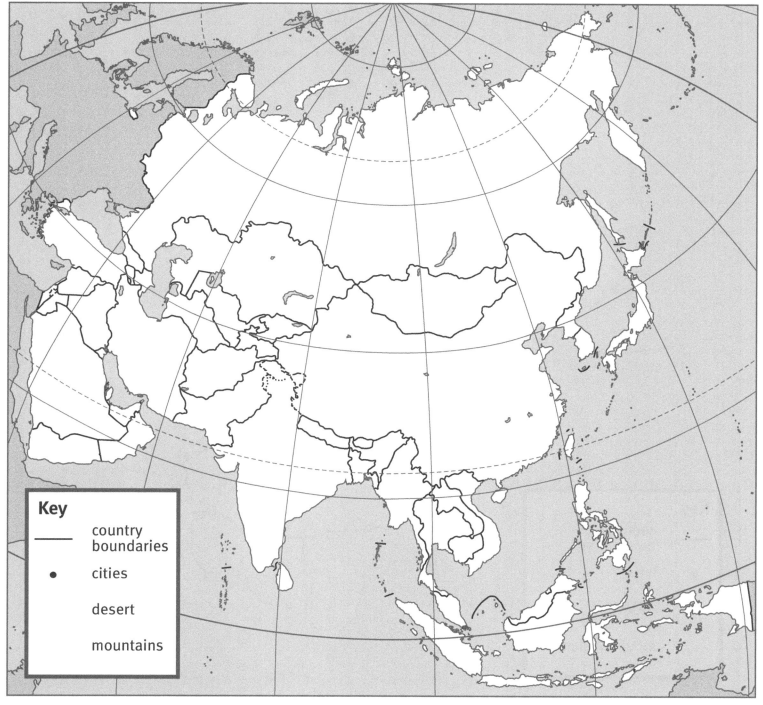

Key

——— country boundaries

• cities

desert

mountains

12 Africa place knowledge

1 Complete the map key.

2 Label these places on the map.
   Remember to use different styles of
   lettering for countries and cities.

NIGERIA	ALGERIA	KENYA
Abuja	Algiers	Nairobi
SOUTH AFRICA	EGYPT	SOMALIA
Pretoria	Cairo	Mogadishu

3 Label these places on the map
   using a different style of lettering
   for deserts and mountains.

Sahara
Kalahari
Mt. Kilimanjaro
Mt. Kenya

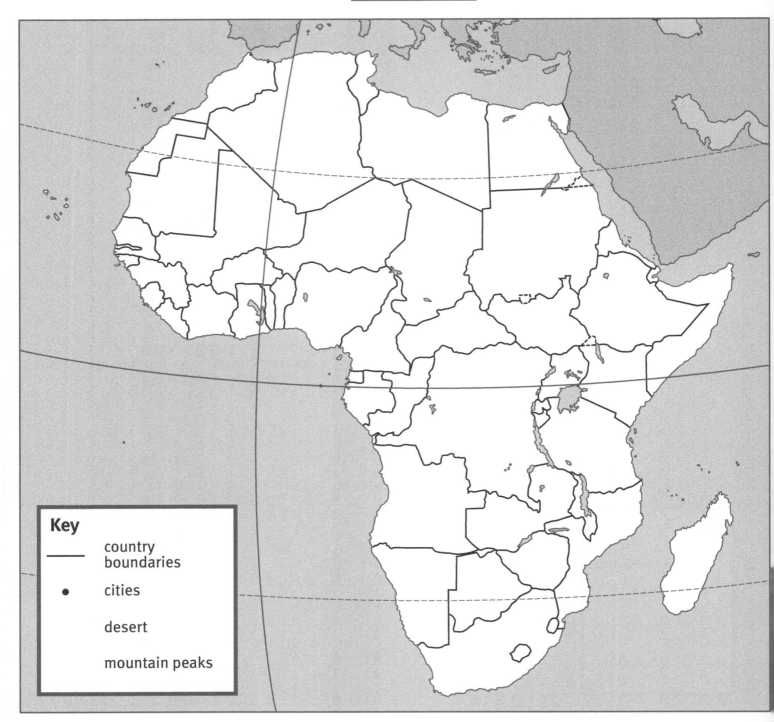

Key

——— country
      boundaries

• cities

   desert

   mountain peaks

1 Complete the map key.

2 Label these places on the map. Remember to use different styles of lettering for countries and cities.

AUSTRALIA	NEW ZEALAND	PAPUA NEW GUINEA
Canberra	Wellington	Port Moresby

3 Label these features on the map using a different style of lettering for deserts and mountains.

Great Dividing Range	Great Sandy Desert
Macdonnell Ranges	Great Victoria Desert
Hammersley Range	Gibson Desert
Maoke Mountains	Simpson Desert

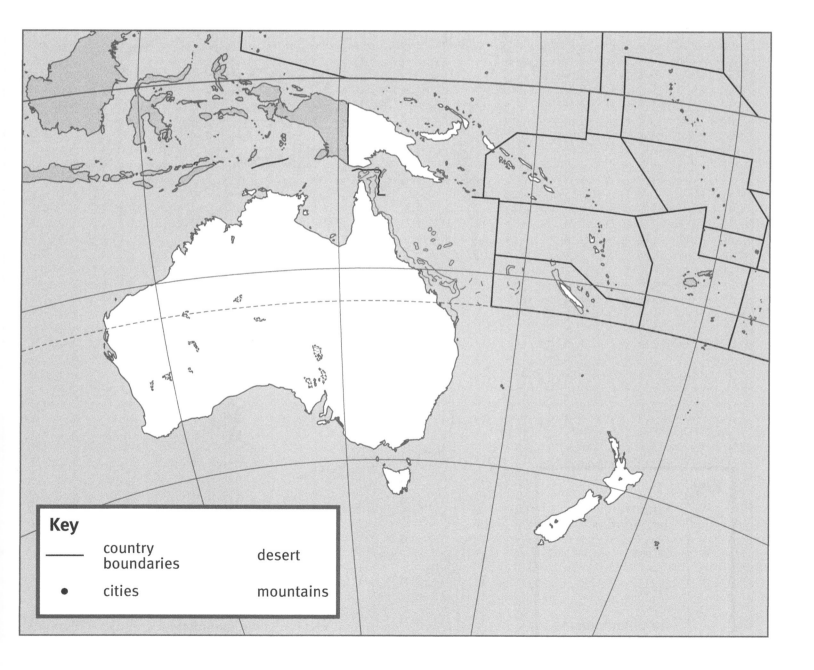

Key

—— country boundaries

• cities

desert

mountains

14 North America place knowledge

1 Complete the map key.

2 Label these places on the map. Remember to use different styles of lettering for countries and cities.

UNITED STATES OF AMERICA (USA)	Los Angeles	MEXICO
Washington DC	San Francisco	Mexico City
New York	CANADA	GREENLAND
Chicago	Ottawa	Nuuk

3 Label these places on the map using a different style of lettering for rivers and mountains.

Rocky Mountains	Missouri
Appalachians	Rio Grande
Mississippi	

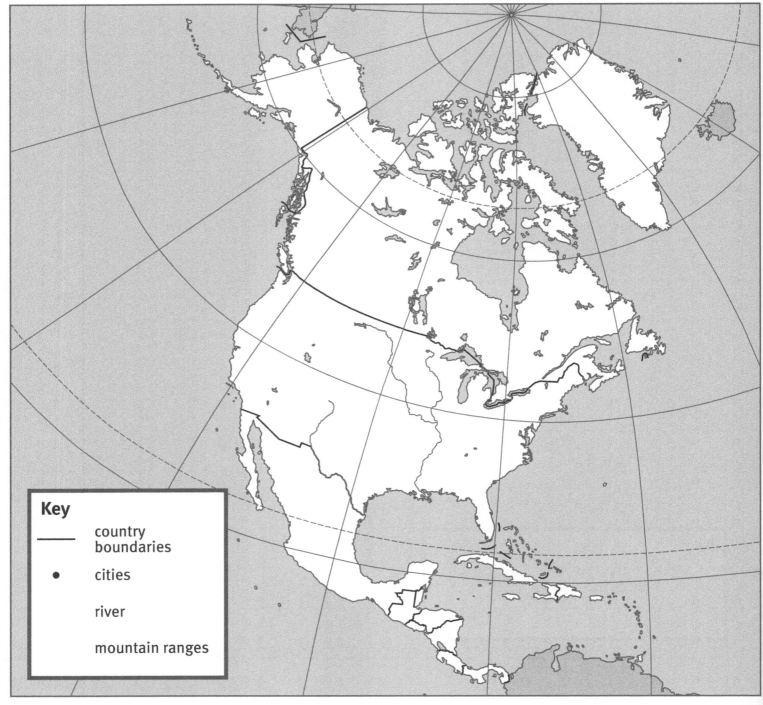

Key

_____ country boundaries

• cities

river

mountain ranges

1 **Complete the map key.**

2 **Label these places on the map. Remember to use different styles of lettering for countries and cities.**

BRAZIL	PERU	URUGUAY
Brásília	Lima	Montevideo
ARGENTINA	VENEZUELA	BOLIVIA
Buenos Aires	Caracas	La Paz
CHILE	COLOMBIA	PARAGUAY
Santiago	Bogotá	Asunción

3 **Label these features on the map using a different style of lettering for mountain range and desert.**

Andes
Atacama Desert

Key

—— country boundaries

• cities

desert

mountain ranges

16 Symbols

1 Here are some everyday symbols.
Write underneath each symbol what it represents.

_____	_____	_____	_____	_____

2 Draw some more examples of everyday symbols and label what they mean.

_____	_____	_____	_____	_____	_____

_____	_____	_____	_____	_____	_____

3 Symbols on maps need to be clear and easily recognised.
In these spaces, design a map symbol for each feature.

volcano	heliport	wildlife park	fruit farm	conservation area	sports centre	supermarket

reservoir	shipbuilding	diamond mine	archaeological site	ski resort	hydro-electric power	computer factory

5 Symbols can be points, lines or areas. Look through your atlas to find examples of each type of symbol.

Complete the table by drawing examples of each symbol. Write their meanings and the atlas page on which they appear.

Point symbols

1	2	3	4
_____	_____	_____	_____
page_____	page_____	page_____	page_____

Line symbols

1	2	3	4
_____	_____	_____	_____
page_____	page_____	page_____	page_____

Area symbols

1	2	3	4
_____	_____	_____	_____
page_____	page_____	page_____	page_____

6 Use your atlas to make a map of your home region. Make sure that there are point, line, and area symbols on the map and in the key.

Key

Map of _____

18 Scale

1 On the maps below, colour the Great Lakes blue. Colour Canada red and the United States of America green.

Atlas maps show scale information like this:

Scale 1: 8 000 000

0   80   160   240   320   400 km

One centimetre on the map represents 80 kilometres on the ground.

2 Complete the scale statements for each of the maps below.

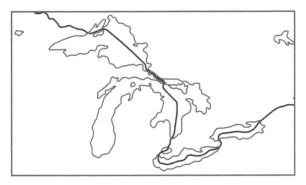

Scale 1: 20 000 000

0   200   400   600   800   1000 km

One centimetre on the map represents _____ kilometres on the ground.

larger scal
smaller area
more detail

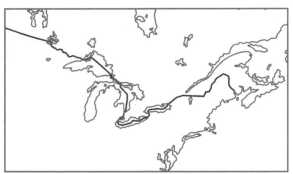

Scale 1: 40 000 000

0   400   800   1200   1600   2000 km

One centimetre on the map represents _____ kilometres on the ground.

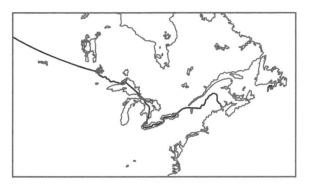

Scale 1: 60 000 000

0   600   1200   1800   2400   3000 km

One centimetre on the map represents _____ kilometres on the ground.

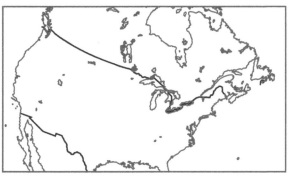

Scale 1: 80 000 000

0   800   1600   2400   3200   4000 km

One centimetre on the map represents _____ kilometres on the ground.

smaller sca
larger area
less detail

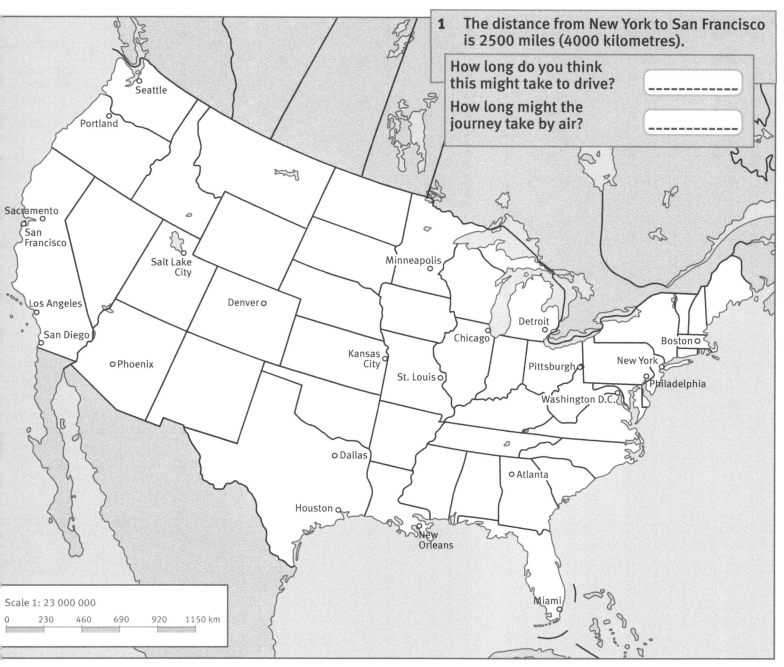

1 The distance from New York to San Francisco is 2500 miles (4000 kilometres).

How long do you think this might take to drive?   _____

How long might the journey take by air?   _____

Seattle
Portland
Sacramento
San Francisco
Los Angeles
San Diego
Phoenix
Salt Lake City
Denver
Minneapolis
Detroit
Chicago
Kansas City
St. Louis
Pittsburgh
New York
Philadelphia
Washington D.C.
Dallas
Atlanta
Boston
Houston
New Orleans
Miami

Scale 1: 23 000 000

0   230   460   690   920   1150 km

2 Use a ruler to measure between Los Angeles and San Diego on the map.

Approximately, how far apart are they in centimetres?   _____

Use the scale information. What distance does this represent on the ground?   _____

3 Use a ruler to measure between Dallas and Kansas City on the map.

Approximately, how far apart are they in centimetres?   _____

Use the scale information. What distance does this represent on the ground?   _____

4 What is the approximate distance on the ground between:

Washington DC and Philadelphia?   _____

Houston and New Orleans?   _____

Pittsburgh and Boston?   _____

Los Angeles and Salt Lake City?   _____

St. Louis and Detroit?   _____

20 Distance

Here is a topographic map of part of Europe at a scale of 1: 11 000 000.

On this map one centimetre represents 110 kilometres on the ground.

Scale 1: 11 000 000

| 0 | 110 | 220 | 330 | 440 | 550 km |

It is approximately 110km between Le Mans and Orléans.

It is approximately 110km between Birmingham and Bristol.

1 Look at the map and find the places in this table.

Estimate the distances between pairs of places and put a tick by the closest estimate.

The distance between				
London and **Southampton** is:	110km	220km	330km	440km
Rennes and **Paris** is:	110km	220km	330km	440km
Frankfurt-am-Main and **Nuremberg** is:	110km	220km	330km	440km
Rotterdam and **Hamburg** is:	110km	220km	330km	440km

Here is a topographic map of part of Asia at a scale of 1: 20 000 000.

On this map one centimetre represents 200 kilometres on the ground.

Scale 1: 20 000 000

| 0 | 200 | 400 | 600 | 800 | 1000 km |

It is approximately 200km between Beijing and Tangshan.

It is approximately 400km between Hefei and Shanghai.

2 Look at the map and find the places in this table.

Estimate the distances between pairs of places and put a tick by the closest estimate.

The distance between				
Hangzhou and **Shanghai** is:	200km	400km	600km	800km
Xi'an and **Zhengzhou** is:	200km	400km	600km	800km
Nanchang and **Shanghai** is:	200km	400km	600km	800km
Xi'an and **Wuhan** is:	200km	400km	600km	800km

The scale line can be used to help estimate the area shown by the map.

diagram A

```
0    10km
├────┤
```

This scale line shows that one centimetre on the map represents ten kilometres on the ground.

```
┌────┐
│    │
└────┘
0    10km
```

One cm^2 on the map, therefore, represents 10km x 10km; that is, 100km^2 on the ground.

4 Look at diagram A.
Using the scale of 1cm to represent 10km, work out what areas are represented by each square.

Write the areas in the spaces provided.

This map shows South Africa at a scale of 1 centimetre to 100 kilometres. Each square centimetre represents 10 000 square kilometres on the ground.

5 You are going to estimate the area of South Africa.

First, tick each square that is entirely filled by South Africa land area.
Then tick those that you estimate to be more than half filled by South Africa. Ignore the rest.

How many squares have you ticked? _____ Now multiply by 10 000 _____

Write your answer here in square kilometres.

Scale 1: 10 000 000

```
0    100   200   300   400   500 km
```

The Earth rotates about an axis that passes through the north and south geographic poles.

Lines of longitude run north–south.

Key

N

arrow points north

1 Draw a north pointer on each meridian of longitude on this view of a globe.

One has been done for you.

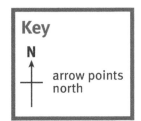

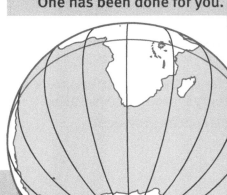

2 Draw a north pointer on each meridian of longitude on this view of a globe.

3 Mark the geographic South Pole on this map with a dot. Label the following on the map: South Africa, South America, Australia.

4 Draw a north pointer on each meridian of longitude on the map.

5 Complete the diagram by writing in the names of the points of the compass.

Use the following abbreviations:

	S	E	W
NE	SE	SW	NW
NNE	ENE	ESE	SSE
SSW	WSW	WNW	NNW

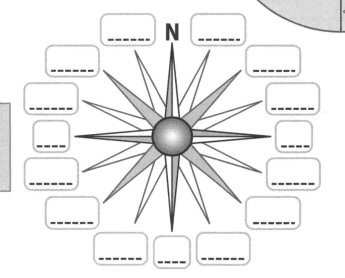

6 Using an atlas map of the United States of America, write in the missing directions.

Arizona is _____ of New Mexico.

Georgia is _____ of Alabama.

Colorado is _____ of Utah.

Oregon is _____ of Washington.

Oklahoma is _____ of Kansas.

South Dakota is _____ of Nebraska.

Nevada is _____ of California.

Wisconsin is _____ of Iowa.

7 Using an atlas map of Africa, write in the missing directions.

Libya is _____ of Chad.

Namibia is _____ of Angola.

Niger is _____ of Nigeria.

Mali is _____ of Mauritania.

Botswana is _____ of the Republic of South Africa.

A B C D E F G H I J K L M N O P Q R S T U V W X Y Z

Place names are listed in the index in alphabetical order.
Australia comes before **Bangladesh**.
Chennai comes before **Delhi**.

1 Write these place names in alphabetical order.
Finland, Egypt, Denmark, Guyana, Canada

place name

----

2 Write these place names in alphabetical order.
Tokyo, Kolkata, Hong Kong, Washington DC, Santiago

place name

When the first letter of the name is the same, you look at the second letter.
Mexico comes before **Mongolia**.
Tanzania comes before **Thailand**.

3 Write these place names in alphabetical order.
Slovakia, Singapore, Samoa, Somalia, Senegal

place name

----

4 Write these place names in alphabetical order.
Portland, Perth, Paris, Pyongyang, Prague

place name

When the second letter is the same,
you look at the third letter, and so on.

5 Write these place names in alphabetical order.
Santiago, Salvador, San Francisco, San Diego, Salt Lake City

place name

----

6 Write these place names in alphabetical order.
South Dakota, South Australia, Southampton South Carolina, South Korea

place name

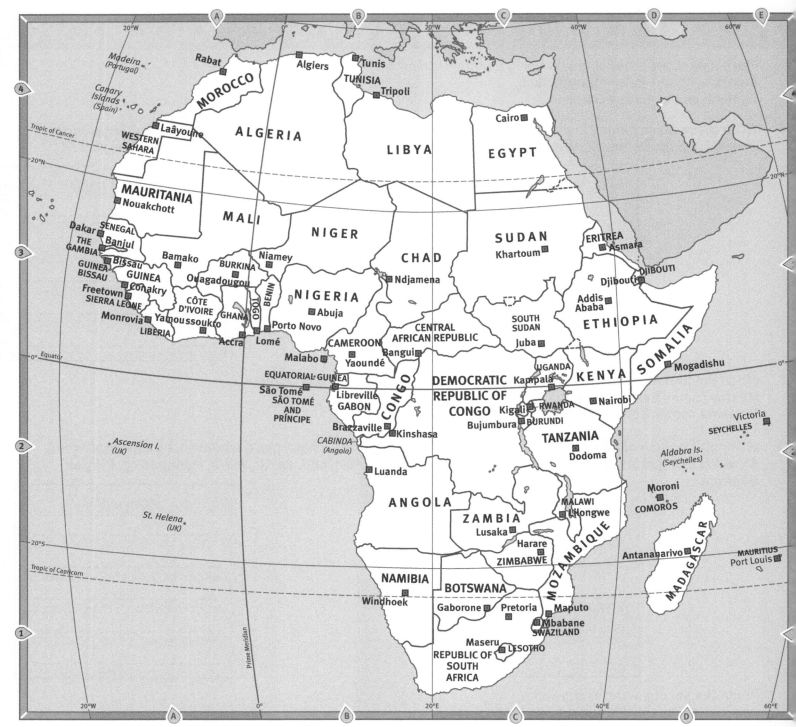

1 In the table, write the names of 5 cities in alphabetical order and the grid code for each city.

City	Grid code

2 In the table, write the names of 5 countries in alphabetical order and the grid code for each country.

Country	Grid code

1 Look up your home town in the atlas index. Complete the index entry for your home town.

name of your home town

_____

page number of atlas map _____

grid code

_____

2 Look at your atlas. Find six islands. Make a mini index of islands. Write the names of the islands in alphabetical order in the table. Complete the table by writing the atlas page number and grid code for each island.

Island mini index		
island	atlas page	grid code
_____	_____	_____
_____	_____	_____
_____	_____	_____
_____	_____	_____
_____	_____	_____
_____	_____	_____

3 Look at your atlas pages. Find six mountain peaks. Make a mini index of mountain peaks. Write the names of the peaks in alphabetical order in the table. Complete the table by writing the atlas page number, grid code and the height of each mountain.

Mountain mini index			
name of peak	atlas page	grid code	height
_____	_____	_____	_____
_____	_____	_____	_____
_____	_____	_____	_____
_____	_____	_____	_____
_____	_____	_____	_____
_____	_____	_____	_____

4 Write the names of these settlements in alphabetical order in the table. Look up each place in the index. Write in the table the page number of the map on which the settlement appears and its grid code. Use the map to find out which river each town stands on.

Montréal
Cairo
Manaus
Varanasi
Budapest
London
Wuhan
Paris

Settlement mini index			
settlement	atlas page	grid code	river
_____	_____	_____	_____
_____	_____	_____	_____
_____	_____	_____	_____
_____	_____	_____	_____
_____	_____	_____	_____
_____	_____	_____	_____
_____	_____	_____	_____
_____	_____	_____	_____

Map reference area 5°N 70°W is shaded like this:

All places in this area share the same reference.

Map reference area 10°S 50°W is shaded like this:

All places in this area share the same reference.

1 Colour the key using a different colour for each map reference.

Locate and colour each area on the map.

Key

☐	0°N 75°W	☐	5°S 60°W
☐	5°N 55°W	☐	10°S 60°W
☐	5°N 75°W	☐	15°S 75°W
☐	0°N 60°W	☐	15°S 45°W

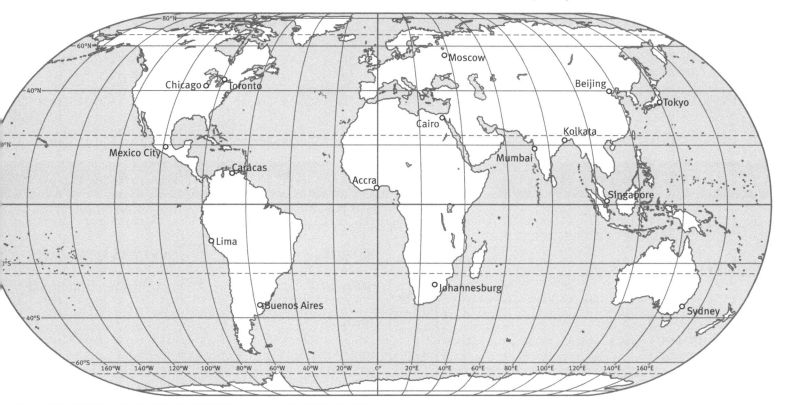

2 Use the lines of latitude and longitude on the map to work out which cities have the following map references:

map reference	city name
19°N 99°W	------------------------
26°S 28°E	------------------------
1°N 103°E	------------------------
43°N 79°W	------------------------
10°N 66°W	------------------------
12°S 77°W	------------------------
39°N 116°E	------------------------
33°S 151°E	------------------------
5°N 0°W	------------------------
22°N 88°E	------------------------
34°S 58°W	------------------------
41°N 87°W	------------------------
30°N 31°E	------------------------
55°N 37°E	------------------------
35°N 139°E	------------------------
18°N 72°E	------------------------

3 Use the map references to locate these cities. Add them to the map.

40°N 73°W	New York
31°N 35°E	Jerusalem
6°S 106°E	Jakarta
31°N 121°E	Shanghai
6°N 3°E	Lagos
23°S 46°W	São Paulo
59°N 30°E	St. Petersburg
28°N 77°E	Delhi
48°N 2°E	Paris
37°N 127°E	Seoul
34°N 118°W	Los Angeles

4 Which is the most northerly city on the map?

Which is the most southerly city on the map?

Locator map

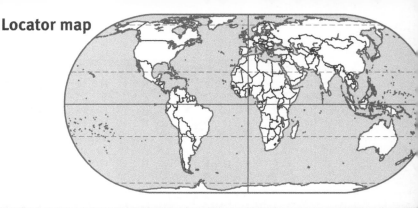

1 Choose a country.
   Colour and name your country on the locator map.

2 Use your atlas to complete the fact file and the questionnaire.

Fact file

capital city _____

major rivers _____
            _____

highest
peaks   _____
            _____

climates   _____
            _____
            _____

environments _____
             _____
             _____

Location questionnaire

Which of the following apply to your chosen country?
(Tick one or more boxes)

☐ landlocked   ☐ northern hemisphere

☐ equatorial   ☐ southern hemisphere

☐ tropical

☐ polar

What is the geographical extent of your chosen country?
(Write numbers of degrees in the boxes)

Most northerly latitude _____

Most southerly latitude _____

Most westerly longitude _____

Most easterly longitude _____

3 Draw a map of your chosen country to show the capital city, other large cities, major rivers, mountain peaks and neighbouring countries.

   Make a key for the map. Give your map a title, north pointer and an approximate scale.

map title _____

Key

Scale:

1 Choose a country.
   Colour and name your country on the locator map.

2 Use your atlas to complete the fact file and the questionnaire.

act file

capital city _____

major rivers _____
_____

highest peaks _____
_____

climates _____
_____
_____

environments _____
_____
_____

Location questionnaire

Which of the following apply to your chosen country?
(Tick one or more boxes)

☐ landlocked   ☐ northern hemisphere

☐ equatorial   ☐ southern hemisphere

☐ tropical

☐ polar

What is the geographical extent of your chosen country?
(Write numbers of degrees in the boxes)

Most northerly latitude   _____

Most southerly latitude   _____

Most westerly longitude   _____

Most easterly longitude   _____

Draw a map of your chosen country to show the capital city, other large cities, major rivers, mountain peaks and neighbouring countries.

Make a key for the map. Give your map a title, north pointer and an approximate scale.

Key

Scale:

map title _____

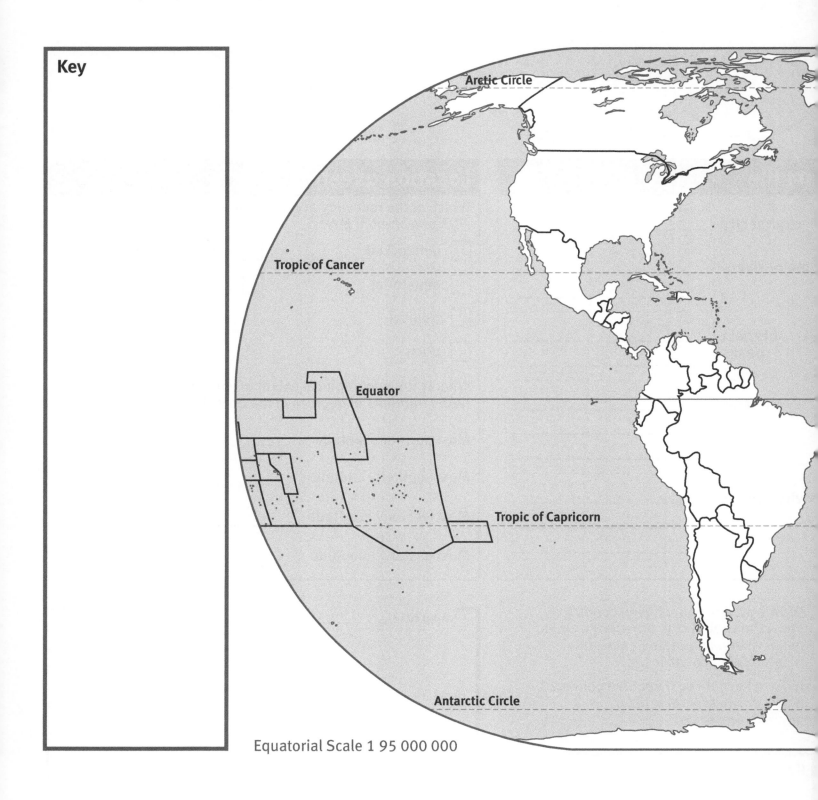

Key

Arctic Circle

Tropic of Cancer

Equator

Tropic of Capricorn

Antarctic Circle

Equatorial Scale 1 95 000 000

Project ideas

Earthquakes, volcanoes, famous buildings, explorers, dinosaurs, space centres, big name clothing brands, gold, silver, diamonds, flags, cars, airlines, menus, songs, stories, permafrost, extreme weather, where people live, where things are made, sports teams, transport, what's in the news, animals, ice, plants, pollution, fishing, tourist attractions, world heritage sites, rich and poor, debt, wars, food, water, disease, endangered species, English language, Spanish language, independence, citrus fruit, floods, droughts, Islam, Christianity,

map title _____

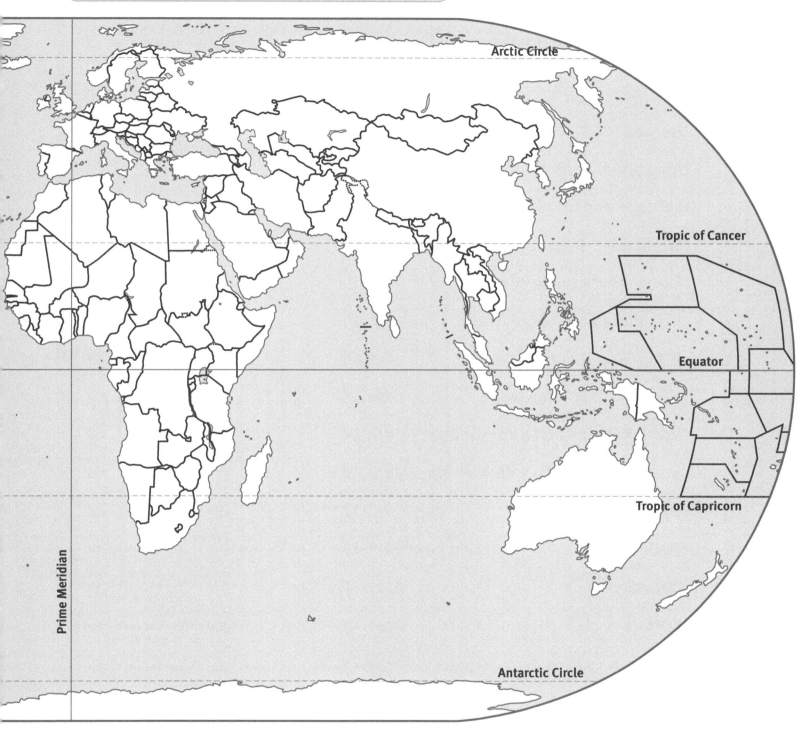

Arctic Circle

Tropic of Cancer

Equator

Tropic of Capricorn

Prime Meridian

Antarctic Circle

laces I'd like to visit, hunger, refugees, terrorism, literacy, transnational corporations, HIV/AIDS, computers, honey, wetlands, migration, trade, fashion centres, motor vehicles, eco-tourism, women's rights, malaria, bund the world races, Greeks, Romans, slavery, World Cup, chocolate, winds and currents, life expectancy, nternet, recycling, shrinking rain forests, spreading deserts, wheat, rice, Olympic Games, whales, fruit and eg from my supermarket, postage stamps . . . .

Progress check

Colour the boxes as you finish each page.

		World map	front cover
		Continents	page 2
		Oceans	page 3
		Map projections	pages 4 – 5
		Latitude and longitude	pages 6 – 7
		World place knowledge	pages 8 – 9
		Europe place knowledge	page 10
		Asia place knowledge	page 11
		Africa place knowledge	page 12
		Oceania place knowledge	page 13
		North America place knowledge	page 14
		South America place knowledge	page 15
		Symbols	pages 16–17
		Scale	pages 18–19
		Distance	page 20
		Area	page 21
		Direction	page 22
		Alphabetical order	page 23
		Grid codes	page 24
		Using the index	page 25
		Geographic coordinates	pages 26–27
		Country file 1	page 28
		Country file 2	page 29
		World project map	pages 30–31

Dr Patrick Wiegand

OXFORD
UNIVERSITY PRESS

Great Clarendon Street, Oxford OX2 6DP

Oxford University Press is a department of the University of Oxford.
It furthers the University's objective of excellence in research, scholarship,
and education by publishing worldwide in

Oxford   New York

Auckland Cape Town Dar es Salaam Hong Kong Karachi
Kuala Lumpur Madrid Melbourne Mexico City Nairobi
New Delhi Shanghai Taipei Toronto

With offices in

Argentina Austria Brazil Chile Czech Republic France Greece
Guatemala Hungary Italy Japan Poland Portugal Singapore
South Korea Switzerland Thailand Turkey Ukraine Vietnam

Oxford is a registered trade mark of Oxford University Press
in the UK and in certain other countries

© Oxford University Press 2012

To accompany the Oxford International Student's Atlas 4th edition

Skills Workbook first published 2007

ISBN: 978 0 19 913758 9

12

Printed in Great Britain by Ashford Colour Press Ltd., Gosport

Oxford International Student's Atlas Skills Workbook
ISBN: 978 0 19 913758 9

Oxford International Student's Atlas
ISBN: 978 0 19 913757 2

How to get in touch:

web   www.oxfordsecondary.co.uk
email   schools.enquiries.uk@oup.com
tel.   +44 (0) 1536 452620
fax   +44 (0) 1865 313472

ISBN 978-0-19-913758-

OXFORD
UNIVERSITY PRESS

ISBN 978-0-19-913758-

9 780199 137589